# "WHEN I WAS YOUR AGE..."

## Remarkable Achievements of Famous Athletes at Every Age from 1 to 100

Written by David Lewman
Illustrated by Mark Anderson

**TRIUMPH**
BOOKS
CHICAGO

This book is available in quantity at special
discounts for your group or organization.
For further information, contact:

Triumph Books
644 South Clark Street
Chicago, Illinois 60605
(312) 939-3330  FAX (312) 663-3557

ISBN 1-57243-145-8

# CONTENTS

when I was a kid, it was important to have a favorite baseball player. Somehow I settled on HARMON KILLEBREW (I think because his nickname was "Killer"), and I carried his card around in my back pocket, ready to pull it out whenever necessary, my official License to Discuss Baseball. Even without referring to the card I could easily recite Killebrew's latest stats: his batting average, his RBIs, his home runs. But I don't think I had any idea how old he was.

# INTRODUCTION

Back then, I simply thought of professional athletes as grown-ups: way older than me, but surely younger than my parents. Now, however, I can be watching a sporting event, completely caught up and enjoying myself, when suddenly, for no reason, I think, "Every player in this game is younger than me." In fact, before too much longer I'll be thinking, "Every player in professional sports is younger than me."

Or will I? When you peruse the pages of this book (starting with your present age), you will be heartened to find that GEORGE BLANDA was still kicking for the NFL at 48, and GORDIE HOWE was still skating for the NHL at 49, and SATCHEL PAIGE was still in there pitching at 59. Consider HARLEY POTTER, who took up golf at 92 and won a golfing medal at 102.

Although it's never too early to take up a sport (gymnasts, skaters, divers, and tennis players have made this point emphatically clear), it can easily be too early to give it up. MICHAEL JORDAN and BILL RUSSELL didn't make their high school basketball teams in their sophomore years. WARREN MOON was passed up in the pro football draft and spent six years playing for the Edmonton Eskimos before he got to the NFL. HOYT WILHELM didn't reach the major leagues until he was 28, but then he stayed for twenty-one seasons.

That's the unpredictable beauty of sports. No matter what age you are, you step out full of potential. And every single time, there's the possibility, no matter how remote, that this hit, this roll, this throw will be a tiny, rare piece of perfection in a world of chaos. Do it often enough, and they may put your picture on a card so some kid can stick it in his pocket.

# THE SINGLE
# DIGITS

# BEING A KID

Future jockey **Willie Shoemaker**, born weighing one pound, thirteen ounces, successfully fights for survival. At birth, **Lew Alcindor** measures a towering twenty-two-and-a-half inches and weighs almost thirteen pounds but doesn't yet call himself "Kareem." Still in diapers, **Greg Louganis**, age 1, joins his older sister's acrobatics class, quickly outperforming the older students. Future NFL quarterback **Todd Marinovich**, age 1, follows his dad's training regimen, which includes push-ups, trying to lift a medicine ball, and teething on a frozen kidney.

At age 2, **Bonnie Blair** puts on her first pair of skates (over her tiny shoes) and steps onto the ice. At the local tennis club where her mother works, **Tracy Austin**, age 2, gets into a program for three- to eight-year-olds. Although he is right-handed, **John Elway**, age 2, hits a whiffle ball lefty because his father makes him. When her mother puts **Julie Krone**, age 2, on a horse, the horse starts to trot away until the future jockey grabs the reins and turns him back. **Secretariat**, age 2, is named Horse of the Year even before he wins the Triple Crown.

# MICHAEL JORDAN

gets airborne for the
first time when he picks up
a frayed extension cord.

**Jimmy Connors**, age 3, starts learning tennis from his mother. **Jennifer Capriati** and **Boris Becker** also both take up tennis at age 3. **Dwight Gooden**, age 3, throws baseballs to the players coached by his father and bats crushed soda cans. Future basketball star **Reggie Miller**, age 3, sleeps with braces on his legs to correct a congenital deformity in his hips. **Pete Rose**, age 3, receives a pair of boxing gloves from his father.

Taking lessons in acrobatics, **Mary Lou Retton**, age 4, masters one-arm front and back walkovers. To prove he's big enough to play with the older boys, future pitcher **Christy Mathewson**, age 4, throws a rag ball over the roof of a barn and through a window. Future track star **Wilma Rudolph**, age 4, nearly dies during a long bout with double pneumonia, scarlet fever, and polio, which leaves her left leg crooked and her foot turned inward.

# WAYNE GRETZKY

makes an
all-star hockey team of
ten- and eleven-year-olds.

At age 5, **Coby Orr** of Littleton, Colorado, hits a hole-in-one. Under the guidance of her father, a medical researcher at the National Institute of Health, **Jennifer Amyx**, age 5, runs her first marathon. Although he is a thin child with chronic bronchial problems, **Jesse Owens**, age 6, helps his parents pick cotton. Future billiards champ **Willie Mosconi**, age 5, sneaks into his father's pool hall to practice with a broomstick and potatoes. While some of her peers started lessons at three, **Martina Navratilova**, age 6, begins tennis lessons with her stepfather in Czechoslovakia.

*At the Austin
country club,*
# BEN CRENSHAW
takes his first
golf lessons.

# GEORGE "THE BABE" RUTH

is deemed "incorrigible" and committed to St. Mary's Industrial School for Boys, where the Catholic brothers teach him baseball.

**Arthur Ashe**, age 7, watches his hometown's best black tennis player practice until the man offers to teach Ashe to play. Ashe says yes. **Cathy Rigby**, age 8, joins a trampoline class and amazes her teacher by doing a back flip the first day. At age 8, **Jackie Robinson** stands up to a racist neighbor across the street. When the man throws rocks at him, Jackie throws them back.

**Vincent Jackson**, age 8, dares his older cousin to punch him in the stomach. When Vincent just laughs off the punch, everyone starts calling him "Boar," later shortened to "Bo." **Bobby Jones**, age 9, beats a sixteen-year-old to win a junior golf tournament. At age 9, British jockey **Frank Wooten** rides his first winner. **Al Unser, Jr.**, age 9, races go-carts.

# THE TEENS

# A TRIP THROUGH ADOLESCENCE

**Sonja Henie**, age 10, wins Norway's figure-skating championship. On horseback at age 10, **Anne Lewis** wins the Women's Professional Rodeo Association's world title for barrel racing. **Andrew Pinetti**, age 10, swims the one and a quarter miles across the Golden Gate strait, from San Francisco to Marin County, in just over half an hour. On his first nine holes ever, **Jack "Golden Cub" Nicklaus** shoots a fifty-one at age 10.

# STUART RACHELS
of Birmingham, Alabama,
qualifies as a
Master chess player.

*Just for the fun of it,*
LOU GEHRIG
swims across the Hudson
River to New Jersey.

**Cassius Clay**, age 12, has his bike stolen. Crying, he wanders into a gym where a policeman is teaching boxing. Wanting to beat up the bike thief, Clay signs up. For Christmas, **Pancho Gonzales**, age 12, receives a fifty-cent tennis racquet from his mother, who hopes to entice him away from more violent sports. It works. Golfer **Nancy Lopez**, age 12, wins the New Mexico Women's Amateur championship. Future world-record-holder **Mary Decker**, age 12, races a quarter mile, a half mile, a mile, a two-mile, and a marathon in one week. Then she has an emergency appendectomy. At age 12, **Ben Hogan** takes up caddying when he discovers it pays more than delivering newspapers.

**Lew Alcindor**, already six feet eight inches at age 13, gets the attention of college basketball scouts. **Lee Trevino**, age 13, drops out of school to work on the grounds crew at a golf course. **Monica Seles**, age 13, turns pro; within four years, she is the number-one ranked woman tennis player. **Tina Smilkstein**, age 13, of Davis, California, pogo-jumps 36,218 times in a row.

# MARIO ANDRETTI
drives in Italy's Formula
Junior Racing.

On *the uneven parallel bars,*
NADIA COMANECI
scores gymnastics'
first perfect ten.

Wearing secondhand army shoes into which he's screwed spikes, golfer **Bobby Jones**, age 14, wins the Georgia amateur championship, qualifying for his first National Amateur. Texan moto-cross racer **Kristi Shealy** becomes her sport's youngest world champion when she wins the Women's World Cup at age 14. **Rebecca Twigg**, age 14, skips high school to go straight to the University of Washington where she takes up competitive cycling.

As a high school sophomore, **Michael Jordan**, age 15, fails to make the varsity basketball team. **Mickey Mantle**, age 15, is kicked in the shin during a football game and gets a staph infection; doctors say his leg will have to be amputated. High school freshman **Earvin Johnson**, age 15, accumulates thirty-six points, eighteen rebounds, and sixteen assists in one game. Afterward, a local sportswriter asks if he can call him "Magic." Earvin, embarrassed, says fine. **Roy Campanella**, age 15, is the starting catcher for the Baltimore Elite Giants in the Negro National League.

*Still in braces,*
# TRACY AUSTIN
turns pro and snaps
Martina Navratilova's
thirty-seven-match
winning streak.

**Joe DiMaggio** quits high school at age 16 to work at an orange juice plant, but hates it. **Dick Fosbury**, age 16, starts developing his "Fosbury Flop," an upside-down high jump that eventually becomes standard. In saloons, **Jack Dempsey**, age 16, challenges all comers and passes the hat after his inevitable victory. At the U.S. swimming championships, **Janet Evans**, age 16, wins the four hundred meter, the eight hundred meter, and the fifteen hundred meter freestyle, as well as the four hundred meter individual medley.

After tying Dizzy Dean's record of seventeen strikeouts in a nine-inning game, Cleveland Indian **Bob Feller**, age 17, heads back to Iowa to finish high school. **Bill Russell** doesn't start playing basketball seriously until his senior year in high school at age 17. Recruited by no one, **Scottie Pippen**, age 17, is accepted at Central Arkansas University on a work-study basis as the basketball team's manager. **Pelé**, age 17, scores six goals to give Brazil soccer's World Cup. **Bob Mathias** wins the Olympic decathlon, the youngest gold medalist ever in that event at age 17.

**Steve Cauthen**, age 18, rides Affirmed to Triple Crown victory. **Hank Aaron**, age 18, drops out of high school to earn two hundred dollars a month playing baseball for the Indianapolis Clowns of the Negro American League. At the University of Georgia, **Herschel Walker**, age 18, gains 1,616 yards (an NCAA record). In his first boxing match, **Joe Louis**, age 18, gets knocked down seven times in two rounds and swears he'll never fight again.

Figure skater **Peggy Fleming**, age 19, wins her fifth consecutive U.S. championship, her third consecutive world championship, and the only gold medal of that year's U.S. Olympic skating team. Although she's made it to the finals at Wimbledon and the French Open, **Andrea Jaeger** quits tennis at age 19. At age 19, **Moses Malone** signs a five-year, three-million-dollar contract with the ABA's Utah Stars, the first player in modern times to go professional right out of high school.

# DWIGHT GOODEN
strikes out two hundred
seventy-six batters,
more than any other pitcher
that year, and more
than any other rookie in
baseball history.

# GERTRUDE EDERLE

swims the English Channel
two hours faster than all of the
men who had done it before
her. When she arrives, a British
customs official checks her
soggy passport.

# THE TWENTIES

# Young
# And
# Adult

Nine years after nervously asking for Kareem's autograph, **Magic Johnson** joins the Lakers at age 20. **Al Travers**, age 20, allows a record twenty-four runs in the only major league game he will ever pitch. **Benjamin Spock** (not yet Dr. Spock, the baby expert) wins a gold medal as a member of the U.S. Olympic rowing team at age 21. Upon graduating from college, **Dave Winfield**, age 21, gets offers from the NFL's Minnesota Vikings, the NBA's Atlanta Hawks, and the ABA's Utah Stars, but decides to play baseball for the San Diego Padres, skipping the minor leagues altogether.

At age 21, **Walter Camp** single-handedly begins to change rugby into football when he proposes hiking the ball from a line of scrimmage. Speed skater **Eric Heiden**, age 21, wins an astonishing five Olympic gold medals, setting three Olympic and two world records. **Jim Palmer**, age 21, pitches a shutout in the World Series, the youngest pitcher to ever do so. As a rookie, **Jim Brown**, age 21, sets a single-game record when he carries the football two hundred thirty-seven yards. During the Olympic tryouts, **Charles Barkley**, age 21, is cut by coach Bobby Knight. Able to throw a softball over a hundred and sixteen mph, **Joan Joyce**, age 21, strikes out Ted Williams in an exhibition game.

*Even though the entire Michigan defense vows to tackle him,*

RED GRANGE

scores touchdowns the first four times he gets the ball in just twelve minutes of play.

In his first pro football game, **Fran Tarkenton**, age 21, relieves the starting quarterback, throws four touchdown passes, and runs one in himself, leading Minnesota to an upset over Chicago. Future star **Warren Moon** is completely passed over in the NFL draft at age 21 and ends up quarterbacking the Edmonton Eskimos for six years. Despite being born without a right hand, **Jim Abbott**, age 21, strikes out a hundred and fifteen batters and pitches two shutouts in his rookie season with the California Angels.

**Wilt Chamberlain**, age 22, joins his first professional basketball team: the Harlem Globetrotters. Future Denver quarterback **John Elway**, age 22, bats .319 for one of the Yankees' minor league teams. **Gary Kasparov**, age 22, becomes the youngest world chess champion in history. In overtime of the final Stanley Cup game, **Bobby Orr**, age 22, scores the winning goal. As a rookie for the Chicago Bears, **Gale Sayers**, age 22, sets a league record (and matches his age) with twenty-two touchdowns, six of them in one game. Although he's drafted by the Knicks, **Bill Bradley**, age 22, passes up the NBA to attend Oxford University on a Rhodes scholarship.

*Much to Hitler's chagrin,* JESSE OWENS wins four gold medals in Berlin.

**Walter Payton**, age 23, breaks O. J. Simpson's record when he rushes for 275 yards in a single game. **Carl Lewis**, age 23, wins four Olympic gold medals, hitting the tape in the one hundred meter at twenty-eight mph. **Oscar Robertson**, age 23, ends his second season with the NBA's first and only "Triple Double," averaging 30.8 points, 12.5 rebounds, and 11.4 assists per game. **Rod Carew**, age 23, sets an American League record when he steals home for the seventh time of the season. **Shaquille O'Neal**, age 23, wins his first scoring crown, averaging 29.3 points a game.

While still playing shortstop, **Lou Boudreau**, age 24, manages the Cleveland Indians. **Chuck Cooper**, age 24, breaks the NBA's color barrier when he joins the Boston Celtics. Quarterback **Sid Luckman**, age 24, provides a stunning argument in favor of the Chicago Bears' new T-formation with a 73–0 win over the Washington Redskins. Frenchman **Philippe Petit**, age 24, walks a wire strung between the World Trade Center's two towers 1,350 feet above the sidewalk. Native American **Jim Thorpe**, age 24, is the first person to win Olympic gold medals for the decathlon and the pentathlon. When he admits to playing semi-pro baseball the summer before, he is stripped of his medals.

# WILT CHAMBERLAIN

scores 100 points in a single game.
His team wins.

**Muhammad Ali**, age 25, refuses to join the army, so he is tried and sentenced to five years in prison. After four years of working in a post office to earn money for college, **Knute Rockne**, age 25, arrives at Notre Dame where he and his quarterback roommate stun West Point with a new trick: the forward pass. British runner **Roger Bannister**, age 25, breaks the four-minute mile. **"Spider Dan" Goodwin**, age 25, climbs up the side of the Sears Tower in Chicago, the world's tallest building. **Joe Namath**, age 25, guarantees that his Jets will beat the heavily favored Colts in Super Bowl III, which they do.

# CHARLES LINDBERGH
lands outside Paris as the first
solo aviator to fly non-stop
across the Atlantic.

**Joe DiMaggio**, age 26, hits safely in fifty-six straight games, a record that has stood for over fifty-five years and counting. **George Halas**, age 26, suggests that the American Professional Football Association change its name to the National Football League and rechristens his own team the Bears. **Richard Petty**, age 26, wins the Daytona 500, the youngest driver to take first place. Gentleman **Jim Corbett**, age 26, becomes the new boxing champion when he knocks out John L. Sullivan in the twenty-first round.

**Eddie Gaedel**, age 26 and three feet seven inches, comes to bat for St. Louis. He gets a walk, goes to first, is replaced by a pinch-runner, and retires from baseball. Football player **Ernie Nevers** sets a solid record at age 26 when he scores all of the Chicago Cardinals' points in a 40–6 victory over the Chicago Bears. **Steffi Graf**, age 26, wins her sixth Wimbledon and her fourth U.S. Open. After her father is arrested for tax evasion, she deposits $14.3 million with German authorities to cover unpaid back taxes. At age 26, **Joe Adcock** hits four home runs and a double in one major league game; no one else ever has.

MUHAMMAD ALI
makes his Broadway
(and theatrical) debut
playing the lead in a musical
called *Buck White*.

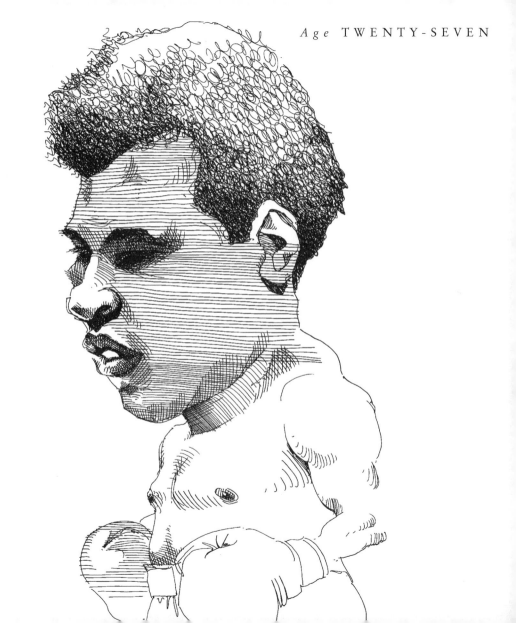

Having finished college and four years of military service, **Roger Staubach**, age 27, finally joins the NFL. At age 27, **Bobby Thomson** fires his "shot heard 'round the world," a pennant-winning homer. After several years as a golf hustler, **Lee Trevino**, age 27, finally joins the PGA tour and is named Rookie of the Year. Having finally broken into the majors, **Maury Wills**, age 27, leads the league with fifty stolen bases in his second season. While battling Hodgkin's disease, **Mario Lemieux**, age 27, ends the hockey season averaging 2.66 points per game, a record second only to Gretzky's.

**Jackie Robinson**, age 28, puts on a Brooklyn Dodgers uniform for the first time. With her husband, **Kathleen Saville**, age 28, rows 10,000 miles across the South Pacific—the longest rowing voyage on record. Returning to tennis after having a baby, **Margaret Smith Court**, age 28, wins three out of four Grand Slam tournaments. Left end **Deacon Jones**, age 28, sacks the quarterback twenty-six times and is named the NFL's Defensive Player of the Year. Rodeo cowboy **Tom Ferguson**, age 28, wins an unprecedented sixth consecutive national all-around championship.

# BILLIE JEAN KING
### wins at Wimbledon
### in singles and
### both doubles, basically
### everything they have.

**Greg LeMond**, age 29, wins his third Tour de France, more than any other American cyclist. **Wayne Gretzky**, age 29, scores his two thousandth goal—the first pro hockey player ever to reach this scoring pinnacle. Having won thirteen major golf championships, including golf's only Grand Slam, **Bobby Jones**, age 29, makes a series of golf instructional films and retires from the game. **Bronko Nagurski**, age 29, retires from the Chicago Bears to try his hand at pro wrestling and soon becomes world champion. **Bobby Fischer**, age 29, beats Boris Spassky to become America's first (and only) world chess champion.

**Althea Gibson**, age 29, is the first black woman to win Wimbledon and the U.S. Open. Cincinnati Red **Johnny Bench**, age 29, is the starting catcher at the All-Star game for his tenth year in a row. Hockey player **Joe Malone**, age 29, scores seven goals in a single game, a record that will stand for seventy-six years (and counting). Despite an arthritic elbow, **Sandy Koufax**, age 29, pitches the fourth no-hitter of his career—his only perfect game. Despite being up the night before with a bad stomachache, **Willie Mays**, age 29, hits four home runs in the first eight innings of a single game.

# THE THIRTIES

# DOWN
## THE
# MIDDLE

*Much to the consternation of folding chairs,* BOBBY KNIGHT arrives as head coach at Indiana University.

*Age* THIRTY

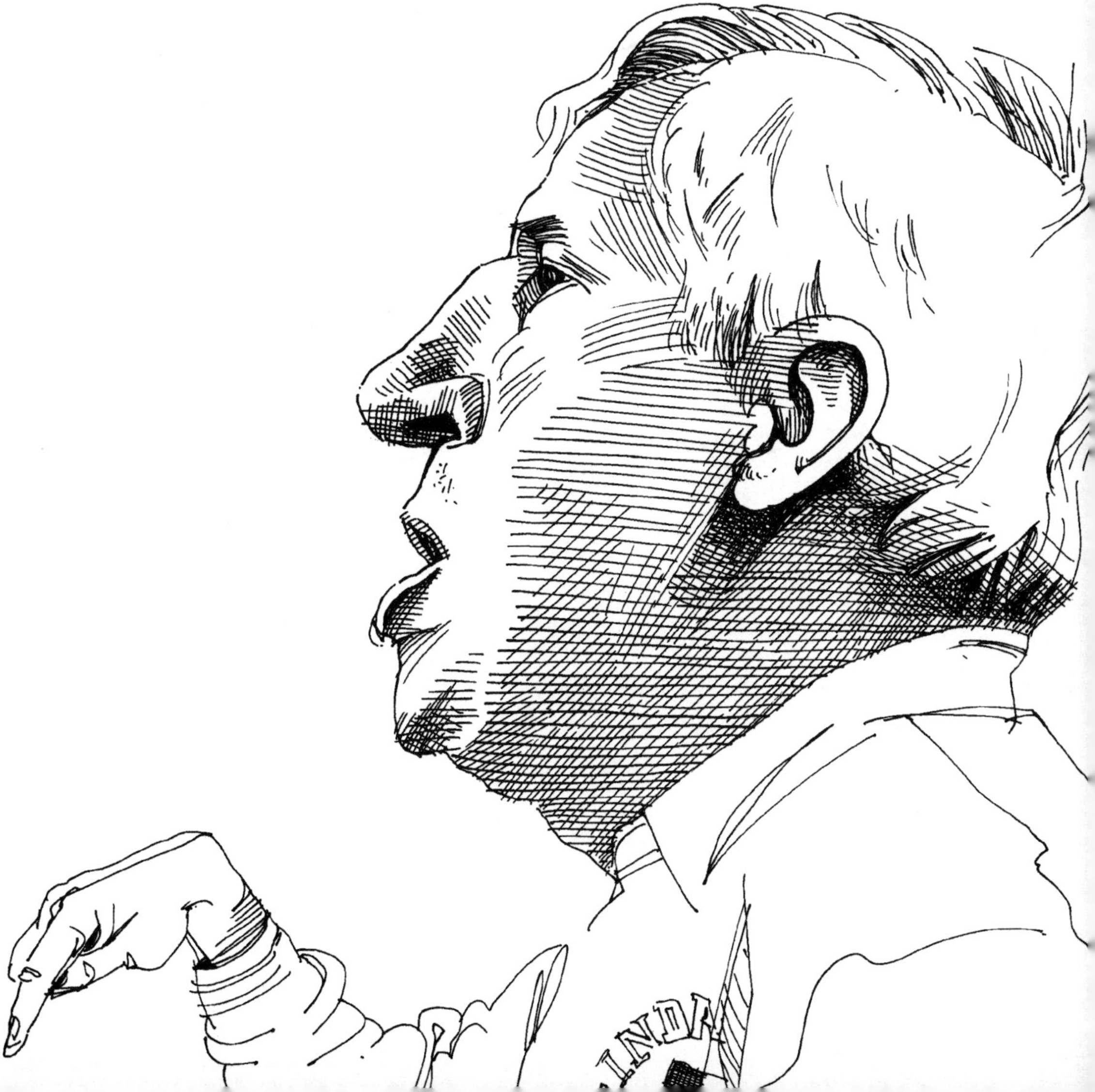

**James Naismith**, age 30, asks the janitor to nail peach baskets up in the gym at the YMCA Training School in Springfield, Massachusetts. Basketball is born. Seven years after winning his first Olympic gold medal, **Carl Lewis**, age 30, sets a new world record, running the one hundred meter dash in just 9.86 seconds. In the last bareknuckle heavyweight championship fight, **John L. Sullivan**, age 30, wins after seventy-five rounds. At age 30, **Walter Payton** breaks Jim Brown's career rushing record of 12,312 yards. **Chris Ford** of the Boston Celtics, age 30, scores the NBA's first official three-point shot.

**Michael Jordan**, age 31, quits basketball to try his hand at professional baseball. At age 31, **Terry Bradshaw** wins his fourth Super Bowl ring, more than any other quarterback. After going undefeated in one hundred twenty-two straight races, **Edwin Moses**, age 31, finally loses a four hundred meter hurdle event. Banned from baseball for life at age 31, **Shoeless Joe Jackson** returns to South Carolina and runs a liquor store. **Chris Evert**, age 31, wins the French Open, her eighteenth Grand Slam title. **Lou Gehrig**, age 31, wins baseball's Triple Crown with a .363 average, forty-nine home runs, and a hundred and sixty-five RBIs. Over two games of the World Series, **Reggie "Mr. October" Jackson** hits four home runs with four consecutive swings.

# BART STARR

sets a new record when
he throws his 294th
consecutive pass without
an interception.
Then he gets intercepted.

After eleven years on the PGA tour, **Ben Crenshaw**, age 32, wins his first major tournament, the Masters. At age 32, **Arthur Ashe** beats a heavily favored Jimmy Connors at Wimbledon, the first black man to win the All-England tournament. Seven years after his title was stripped for refusing to go to Vietnam, **Muhammad Ali**, age 32, beats Joe Frazier and George Foreman to regain the world championship. **Bob Gibson**, age 32, sets a new record when he strikes out seventeen batters in a World Series game. At age 32, **Bill Russell** leads the Boston Celtics to their eighth straight NBA championship and then becomes the team's player-coach, the first black coach in NBA history.

At age 32, heavyweight champ **Rocky Marciano** wins his forty-ninth professional fight (out of forty-nine) and retires. At age 32, **Magic Johnson** finds out he is HIV-positive and retires from the Lakers, but he plays in the All-Star game and with Larry Bird in the Olympics. **Catfish Hunter**, age 32, pitches his forty-second shutout. **Eric Dickerson**, age 32, retires with 13,259 rushing yards, second only to Walter Payton. **Buzz Arlett**, age 32, finally gets to play in the majors; although he hits .313 with fifty-one extra-base hits, he's sent back to the minors and never plays in the major leagues again.

Edmund Hillary, age 33, reaches the top of Mount Everest. When he takes over the Baltimore Colts at age 33, Don Shula becomes the youngest coach in pro football. After playing baseball for the Chicago White Sox, Billy Sunday, age 33, decides to become a preacher. Martina Navratilova wins her ninth women's singles crown at Wimbledon at age 33. Buffalo quarterback Jim Kelly, age 33, wins his fourth consecutive AFC championship and loses his fourth consecutive Super Bowl.

**Pelé** comes out of retirement at age 34 to play soccer for the New York Cosmos. The lure? A seven-million-dollar contract. **John Riggins**, age 34, scores twenty-four touchdowns in a single season, more than any other pro football player. Olympic boxer **Eddie Eagan**, age 34, wins another gold medal—as a member of the American bobsledding team. **Arnold Palmer**, age 34, wins his fourth Masters, giving him more green jackets than any other golfer. **Ted Williams**, called back to active service in Korea by the Marines at age 34, lands his jet without landing gear after being shot at.

*Wooden racquet in hand,*
BJORN BORG
attempts and fails a
comeback eight years after
his retirement.

Baltimore Oriole shortstop **Cal Ripken, Jr.**, age 35, plays in his 2,131st consecutive game, becoming baseball's new Ironman. **Susan Butcher**, age 35, wins an unprecedented fourth Iditarod Trail sled dog race in record time. Having come out of retirement, **Bronko Nagurski**, age 35, scores the touchdown that puts the Chicago Bears ahead in their NFL championship victory over the Washington Redskins. Annie Moses outshoots Frank Butler, joins his traveling show, and at age 35 becomes **Annie Oakley**. At 35, an age that is geriatric by gymnastic standards, **Agnes Keleti** of Hungary wins three Olympic gold medals. Former Knick **Bill Bradley**, age 35, wins election to the U.S. Senate.

On the Fourth of July, **Lou Gehrig**, age 36, says farewell to the Yankee fans. **John Riggins**, age 36, retires from football, having gained more yards in his thirties than he did in his twenties. When the home plate umpire collapses in the heat, White Sox outfielder **Jocko Conlan**, age 36, takes over. Praised for his fairness, he switches to umpiring permanently and eventually makes the Hall of Fame. The last player to shoot free throws underhanded, **Rick Barry**, age 36, hits 93.5 percent from the charity stripe to lead the league. At age 36, **Bill Buckner** of the Red Sox lets a grounder go through his legs, losing a World Series game to the Mets, who go on to take the championship. In his final season, playing with almost no cartilage left in his knees, **Mickey Mantle**, age 36, manages to hit eighteen home runs.

*Lawyer*

# HOWARD COSELL

becomes a full-time sports
reporter for ABC.

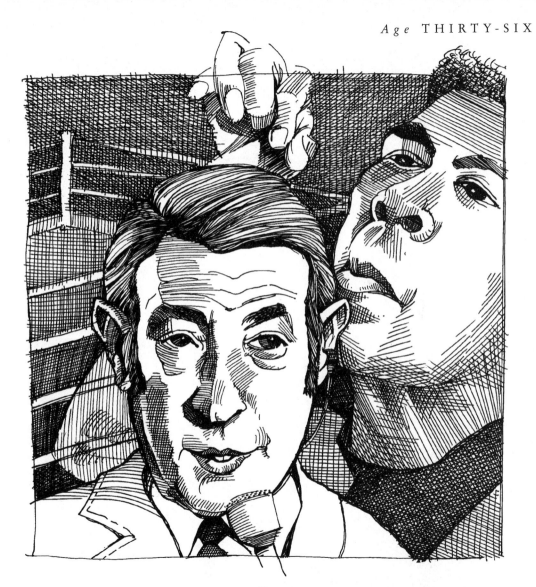

*Less than two years
after breaking his ankle,
pelvis, and collarbone
in a car accident, golfer*
BEN HOGAN
wins the U.S. Open.

In the World Series, taunted by jeering fans and the opposing team, **Babe Ruth**, age 37, indicates that his next swing will send the ball into the stands. And it does. **Sugar Ray Robinson**, age 37, beats Carmen Basilio to regain the middleweight title, thus becoming the only fighter to win a championship five times. **Mark Allen** of Boulder, Colorado, wins his sixth Ironman triathlon at age 37. **Dennis Conner**, age 37, wins his first America's Cup as skipper of *Freedom*. In the bathyscaphe *Trieste*, **Jacques Piccard**, age 37, dives down 35,800 feet into the Pacific Ocean's Mariana Trench.

When his second baseman leaves to help fight World War Two, manager **Leo Durocher**, age 38, takes over himself and breaks his thumb on a bad throw from the shortstop. **Ted Turner**, age 38, wins the America's Cup in his yacht, *Courageous*. **Woody Hayes** begins coaching football at Ohio State at age 38. **Roberto Clemente**, age 38, bangs out a double, his three thousandth—and last—hit. Three months later he dies in a plane crash.

YOGI BERRA
plays in his seventy-fifth
World Series game,
a record.

**Roald Amundsen**, age 39, beats Robert F. Scott to the South Pole. **Phil Esposito**, age 39, makes his 717th goal and 873rd assist, landing fourth on hockey's all-time list of scorers. In his fifteenth season of major-league baseball, Milwaukee Brave **Warren Spahn**, age 39, pitches his first no-hitter. **Walter Johnson**, age 39, pitches his one hundred and tenth shutout, a record that will stand for sixty-nine years (and counting). Seven years after retiring from pro basketball, **"Pistol" Pete Maravich**, age 39, plays a pickup game, has a heart attack, and dies. **Raisa Smetanina**, Soviet cross-country skier age 39, wins her tenth Olympic medal and her fourth gold.

# TED WILLIAMS
out-hits Mickey Mantle
to become the oldest winner
of the batting title with
a .388 average.

# THE FORTIES

# FORGING
# AHEAD

*After running the numbers
game in Cleveland and
serving four years
in prison,*
DON KING
becomes a boxing
manager and promoter.

**Terry Sawchuk**, age 40, wins his four hundred thirty-fifth hockey game, more than any other goalie. At home after the season, Sawchuk fights a teammate and dies from the resulting injuries. Riding Fabius, **Eddie Arcaro**, age 40, wins a record sixth Preakness. **Frank Robinson** becomes the first black manager in the major leagues at age 40. **James Edwards**, age 40, gets to play on his seventh NBA team, the Chicago Bulls, who win more games in the regular season than any other team in history. In his first season at Michigan, **Bo Schembechler**, age 40, snaps his former coach's twenty-two game winning streak when the Wolverines upset Woody Hayes's Ohio State squad. **George Brett**, age 40, hits thirty-one doubles, lifting him to fifth on the all-time list.

Billiards champ **Willie Mosconi**, age 41, pockets five hundred twenty-six balls without a miss. **Pancho Gonzales**, age 41, beats a twenty-five-year-old in a five-hour, one-hundred-and-twelve-game match, the longest ever played at Wimbledon. Seattle Mariner **Ken Griffey**, age 41, rooms with a player he knows pretty well: his son, Ken Griffey, Jr. **Gerhard Weidner**, age 41, sets a world record for the twenty-mile walk, making him the oldest athlete to set a world record open to all ages. **Jimmy Connors**, age 41, retires from tennis with a hundred and nine tournament victories, more than any other player.

*Former All-Pro tight end*
MIKE DITKA
returns to the
Chicago Bears as head coach.

**Satchel Paige**, age 42, finally pitches his first full game in the major leagues, a shutout against the Chicago White Sox. A week later, he does it again. **Kareem Abdul-Jabbar**, age 42, scores his 38,387th point as a pro, setting an all-but-invincible record. **A. J. Foyt**, age 42, wins a record fourth Indy 500. After undergoing surgery for cancer, **Babe Didrikson Zaharias**, age 42, wins the U.S. Women's Open by twelve strokes. In his twentieth NBA season, **Robert Parish**, age 42, plays his 1,561st game, beating Kareem Abdul-Jabbar's all-time record. **Stan "the Man" Musial**, age 42, gets his 3,630th hit, bats in his 1,951st runner, and also becomes a grandfather.

*At age 43,*
# JACKIE ROBINSON
is the first black baseball player to be elected to the Hall of Fame.

JANE FONDA
publishes her workout
book, which becomes
one of the biggest
hardcover best-sellers
in history.

**Cy Young**, age 44, strikes out his 2,799th batter to end his career with more wins (and more losses) than any other major league pitcher. **Phil Jackson**, age 44, lands his first head coaching job in the NBA with the Chicago Bulls. It works out well. **Pete Rose**, age 44, gets his 4,192nd hit, breaking Ty Cobb's long-standing record. At age 44, **Bear Bryant** takes over as head football coach for his old college team, the University of Alabama. **Nolan Ryan**, age 44, pitches his seventh no-hitter.

**Kathy Whitworth** wins her eighty-eighth tournament at age 45, more than any other pro golfer, male or female. Heisman Trophy–winner **Peter Dawkins**, age 45, becomes the Army's youngest general. **Tommy John**, age 45, bobbles, throws wild to first, and then throws wild to home for a record three errors in one play. The Yankees win anyway.

VINCE LOMBARDI
lands his first head coaching
job in the NFL with the
Green Bay Packers.

**George Foreman**, age 46, knocks out Michael Moorer in the tenth round to become the oldest boxing champ in any weight division. As a pitcher for St. Louis at age 46, **Satchel Paige** hurls ninety-one strikeouts, two shutouts, and leads the league in games won as a reliever (eight). He also leads the league in games lost as a reliever (eight). South African **Susan Fraenkel**, age 46, swims the English Channel in twelve hours and five minutes.

**Al Unser** becomes the Indy 500's oldest champion at age 47. **Ben Hogan**, age 47, shoots a record thirty on the back nine at the Masters. Because he has bet heavily on horses, dogs, and possibly baseball players, **Pete Rose**, age 47, is banned from baseball for life. He pleads guilty to income tax evasion and is sentenced to five months in prison.

At the end of his twenty-six season career (the longest in pro football history), **George Blanda** scores his 2,002nd point at age 48, setting a record that is over three hundred points higher than the runner-up. **Phil "Knucksie" Niekro**, age 48, pitches his 318th win and his 3,342nd strikeout. **Red Auerbach**, age 48, coaches the Celtics to their eighth straight NBA championship.

After twenty years of seclusion, **Bobby Fischer**, age 49, beats Boris Spassky again, this time for over three million dollars. Thanks to his knuckleball, **Hoyt Wilhelm**, age 49, pitches his 1,070th game, more than any other major leaguer. American **Jay O'Brien**, age 49, wins an Olympic gold medal as a member of the four-man bobsled team.

*Having retired six years
before and played for
the World Hockey Association
in between,*
GORDIE HOWE
returns to the NHL.

# THE FIFTIES

# SECOND
# WIND

**Bobby Allison**, age 50, wins the Daytona 500. At age 50, **Sparky Anderson** is the first manager to win World Series championships in both the National and American leagues. When the Miami Heat offers **Pat Riley**, age 50, a coaching job and part-ownership, he jumps to his third NBA team. Former slugger **Ted Williams**, age 50, begins a new chapter in his baseball career, managing the Washington Senators.

Even though it means banishment from all future employment in major league baseball, **Mickey Mantle**, age 51, takes a job as a greeter at the Claridge Casino in Atlantic City. **Lou Holtz**, age 51, coaches Notre Dame to an undefeated season and a national championship. Manager **Billy Martin**, age 51, is rehired by the Yankees but loses his job when he sucker-punches a marshmallow salesman in a hotel lobby. Almost four years after suffering multiple injuries in an accident, jockey **Angel Cordero, Jr.**, age 51, returns to set a new track record at Puerto Rico's El Commandante. **Jim Brown**, age 51, founds Amer-I-Can, a program dedicated to reintegrating gang members into society.

# ARNOLD PALMER

negotiates an agreement
to build the first
golf course in China.

Georgetown coach **John Thompson**, age 52, leads a threatened boycott by the Black Coaches' Association if the NCAA doesn't allow Division I schools to add a fourteenth basketball scholarship. **Robert E. Peary**, age 52, plants an American flag at the North Pole. **Sam Snead**, age 52, wins the Greater Greensboro Open, the oldest golfer to win a PGA tournament.

As a designated hitter for the White Sox, **Minnie Minoso** gets a single at age 53—the oldest player to hit safely in the majors. By winning the Valvoline 200 at the Phoenix International Raceway, **Mario Andretti**, age 53, becomes the oldest IndyCar race winner. At age 53, Judge **Kenesaw Mountain Landis** becomes the first commissioner of baseball and bans the eight Chicago "Black Sox" from the game for life. Fighting cancer, **the Babe**, age 53, makes his final appearance in Yankee Stadium for the twenty-fifth anniversary of "The House That Ruth Built" and receives a huge ovation.

*Still fiercely competitive,*
TY COBB
beats Babe Ruth two matches
out of three in a charity
golf tournament.

Retired baseball player **"Orator Jim" O'Rourke**, age 54, talks the Giants' manager into letting him play one more game. He catches the whole game against Cincinnati and even scores a run. Aviatrix **Jacqueline Cochran**, age 54, sets a women's air speed record of 1,429 mph. At age 54, coach **Tom Landry** takes his Dallas Cowboys to a record fifth Super Bowl. Former Wimbledon champ **Bobby Riggs**, age 55, challenges Billie Jean King to a "Battle of the Sexes" but loses in straight sets. As president of the Brooklyn Dodgers, **Branch Rickey**, age 55, brings Jackie Robinson into the major leagues. **Richard Petty**, age 55, drives in his last NASCAR race, finishing his career with two hundred wins, ninety-five more than any other driver.

At age 56, **Captain Joseph Kittinger** crosses the Atlantic Ocean in a balloon before any other solo balloonist. Thanks to endorsements, **Arnold Palmer**, age 56, is still the world's highest-paid athlete, according to *Sport* magazine. Because of his wife's poor health, **Dizzy Dean**, age 57, turns down invitations to run for governor of Mississippi. **Billy Martin**, age 57, becomes the Yankees' manager for the fourth time, until he punches one of his pitchers. **Joe Louis**, age 57, works as a Caesar's Palace greeter, where his duties include signing autographs and playing blackjack with chips provided by the casino.

WILLIE SHOEMAKER
rides in his 40,350th race.
He has won 8,833 races,
more than any other jockey.

As a front-office executive for the Atlanta Braves, **Hank Aaron**, age 58, calls for an investigation into racist remarks by Cincinnati Reds owner Marge Schott. **Doc Counsilman**, an Olympic swim coach, becomes the oldest person, at age 58, to swim the English Channel.

As a Kansas City A, **Satchel Paige**, age 59, pitches three scoreless innings against the Boston Red Sox, allowing just one hit. **Don Kellner**, age 59, jumps out of a plane for the twenty-one thousandth time, more than any other sport parachutist. **Ike Rude**, age 59, wins the steer roping title to become rodeo's oldest world champion.

# THE SIXTIES

# BECOMING REMARK-ABLE

Ramon Blanco of Spain climbs to the top of Mount Everest at age 60. **Cammie Brewer**, age 61, pulls the arm on a Reno slot machine and wins $6,814,823.48. To celebrate the bicentennial, **Jack LaLanne**, age 61, swims towing thirteen boats carrying seventy-six people through Long Beach Harbor.

Basketball coach **Chuck Daly**, age 62, moves from the Pistons to the Nets. In between, he gets to coach the Olympic Dream Team. **Leo Durocher**, age 62, brings the Cubs up from last place to third and is named Manager of the Year. During the Gulf War, Reds owner **Marge Schott**, age 62, dedicates the World Series to "our wonderful women and men over in the Far East."

*Shooting traps,*
ANNIE OAKLEY
hits one hundred
targets in a row.

**Mickey Mantle**, age 63, gets a new liver. Pitcher-turned-announcer **Dizzy Dean**, age 63, calls his last baseball game, sitting in as a guest announcer for NBC. During the broadcast, he praises Bob Gibson for throwing the right pitch "ninety-nine times out of ten." **Bob Feller**, age 63, returns to spring training as a pitching coach for the Indians.

As a member of the Swedish shooting team, **Oscar Swahn**, age 64, is the oldest male Olympian to win a gold medal. **John Wooden**, age 64, coaches UCLA to a tenth national championship and becomes the only coach with more than four NCAA basketball crowns.

*After coaching the
Dallas Cowboys
to twenty-one winning
seasons in a row,*
TOM LANDRY
has three straight losing
seasons and is fired.

Ohio State football coach **Woody Hayes** is forced to resign at age 65 after he attacks an opposing team's player on national television. **Jim Gillcrist**, age 65, high jumps five feet two inches, a record for his age group at the Senior Olympics. To celebrate his birthday, swimmer **Jack LaLanne**, age 65, tows sixty-five boats carrying sixty-five hundred pounds of wood pulp across mile-wide Lake Ashinoko at the base of Mount Fuji.

*Basketball great*
# BOB COUSY
plays an athletic
director in
the movie *Blue Chips*.

In Austin, Minnesota, **Evelyn Culbert**, age 66, bowls a perfect game, the oldest woman on record to do so. Australian **Bertram Clifford Batt**, age 67, swims the English Channel in eighteen hours, thirty-seven minutes. **Pop Warner**, age 67, finishes his football coaching career at Temple with an overall record of three hundred thirteen wins, one hundred and six losses, and thirty-two ties. With partner Vitas Gerulaitis, **Bobby Riggs**, age 67, challenges Martina Navratilova and Pam Shriver to a doubles match. The men lose miserably.

Former Olympian **Boo Morcom**, age 68, sets a record when he pole vaults eleven feet five inches in the Senior Olympics. In the regular Olympics, **Samuel Duvall**, age 68, wins a silver medal for archery. Manager **Casey Stengel**, age 68, leads the New York Yankees to their seventh World Series championship.

*After twenty-five seasons,*
BEAR BRYANT
retires as head coach at
Alabama, having led his
teams to a record fifteen
major bowl wins.

*Age* SIXTY-NINE

# THE SEVENTIES

# ANOTHER KIND OF PRIME TIME

PAUL NEWMAN
becomes the oldest driver to
win a professionally sanctioned
race when he co-drives a
Mustang at Daytona.

**Mavis Lindgren** runs her first marathon at age 70. At the Senior Olympics, **Edith Mendyka**, age 70, runs one hundred meters in under twenty seconds, setting a record for women her age. She also long jumps and throws a discus, a javelin, and a shot put. **Edward Payson Weston**, age 71, walks across the United States—nearly four thousand miles.

**George Halas**, age 72, coaches the Chicago Bears to their three hundred and twenty-fifth victory under his guidance. **Tom Amberry**, age 73, sets a new record when he makes over two thousand free throws in a row. Having won ten pennants with the New York Yankees, **Casey Stengel**, age 73, loses a record one hundred and twenty games in his first season managing the New York Mets. Badminton player **David Field**, age 73, competes in the Senior Olympics while on his honeymoon. **Walt Stack**, age 73, completes the Ironman Triathlon.

*At the first Olympic
basketball game,*
JAMES NAISMITH,
the game's inventor,
tosses the ball up for the
opening tipoff.

**Ty Cobb**, age 74, throws out the first ball at the home opener of the new Los Angeles Angels. It is the last baseball game he will attend. **Henri Soudieres**, age 74, power lifts a total of seven hundred and ninety pounds. **Eddie Robinson**, age 75, enjoys his three hundred eighty-eighth victory as coach of Grambling College's football team. Having taken up cycling after retirement, **Ed Delano**, age 75, rides thirty-one hundred miles in thirty-three days to attend his fiftieth college reunion.

Korean runner **Ki Chung Sohn**, age 76, carries the Olympic torch to open the games in Seoul, fifty-two years after his record-breaking marathon time was credited to occupying Japan. **Leo Durocher**, age 76, gets a divorce when he starts trying to gamble with his wife's money.

**Finis Mitchell**, age 77, climbs his two hundred and fifty-first mountain peak in western Wyoming's Wind River range. Cubs sportscaster **Harry Caray**, age 77, celebrates his fiftieth season in the broadcaster's booth. **Marvin Miller**, age 77, who ended baseball's reserve clause, continues to advise the baseball player's association.

# DELVIN MILLER
begins his sixty-second year
of driving harness races—
the longest career of any
professional athlete.

*A former pitcher in the Negro Leagues,*
LEON DAY
achieves his lifelong dream:
induction into the
Hall of Fame.
Six days later,
he dies a happy man.

At age 78, **Woody Strode**, who broke football's color barrier with Kenny Washington at UCLA, appears in the movie *Storyville*—one of his sixty-plus films. **Joe DiMaggio**, age 79, sits in a room at the Louisville Slugger factory, signs about sixteen hundred bats, and takes home close to two million dollars. **Asa Long** wins his sixth U.S. checkers national title at age 79, the oldest checkers champ ever.

# THE EIGHTIES

# FOR THE INTREPID ONLY

**Mrs. Sylvia Brett** of England sets an age record when she parachutes out of a plane solo at age 80. **Joseph Bruno**, age 80, swims across the Golden Gate strait for the sixty-first time. After thirty-seven years out of the cockpit, **Mary Victor Bruce**, age 81, flies a loop-the-loop. At age 81, **Jerry Wehman** of Port Saint Lucie, Florida, bowls three hundred, the oldest person ever to bowl a perfect game. Coaching football at the College of the Pacific, **Amos Alonzo Stagg**, age 81, is named Coach of the Year.

**William Ivy Baldwin**, age 82, walks across a three-hundred-and-twenty-foot wire stretched across the South Boulder Canyon in Colorado, a drop of a hundred twenty-five feet. **Fred Lasby**, age 82, flies solo around the world in his single-engine Piper Comanche. Legendary broadcaster **Red Barber**, age 83, cheerfully begins his sixty-first year behind the mike, chatting every Friday morning on National Public Radio.

**Avery Brundage**, age 84 and president of the International Olympic Committee, declares "the Games must go on" after terrorist attacks. **Red Grange**, age 84, walks his Chihuahua, Frito, and lives in a house devoid of memorabilia, saying, "Legend to me means nothing." **Marian Hart**, age 84, flies solo across the Atlantic Ocean in a single-engine plane.

# JOHN A. KELLEY
## runs his
## sixty-first
## Boston Marathon.

**Amos Alonzo Stagg**, age 85, joins the football coaching staff of the Susquehanna Crusaders and signs a ten-year contract. As general manager of Churchill Downs, **Colonel Matt Winn**, age 85, oversees his forty-fourth Kentucky Derby. The last British player to win the men's singles title at Wimbledon, **Fred Perry**, age 85, covers the Australian Open for the BBC.

*As founder of the
Pittsburgh Steelers,*
ART ROONEY
continues to run
the team.

*Sixty years after buying
a spiral red notebook to
jot down his teaching
ideas, golf pro*
HARVEY PENICK,
writes his first instruction
guide, *The Little Red Book,*
which quickly sells over
a million copies.

# CONNIE MACK

manages the Philadelphia Athletics
for a fiftieth season.
He finishes his career with
more wins—3,776—
and more losses—4,025—
than any other manager.

GEORGE HALAS
actively advises his
Chicago Bears as a
coaching consultant.

# EDWIN C. TOWNSEND
parachutes out of a plane,
the oldest man
to sky-dive solo.

# The Nineties
# ...and After

# HEADING TOWARD THE CENTURY MARK

**Rose Monda**, age 90, sets five Senior Olympic records in track and field. **Gustave Langer**, age 90, sets six Senior Olympic swimming records. Forty-one years after founding his own company, **Enzo Ferrari**, age 90, supervises race car operations. **Hulda Crooks**, age 91, climbs Mount Whitney, the highest mountain in the continental United States. **George Sayler**, age 91, performs a tandem parachute jump over Snohomish, Washington.

Future Senior Olympic champion **Harley Potter** of Winston-Salem, North Carolina, learns how to golf at age 92. **Paul Spangler**, age 92, completes his fourteenth marathon. At age 93, **Tom Lane** of California practices his backstroke for the state's senior competition. He also throws the discus over twenty-seven feet, the javelin over twenty-six feet, and the shot put over ten feet.

# MICHAEL JORDAN
returns to the
Chicago Bulls and leads the
league in scoring (we hope).

**Erna Ross**, age 95, gets a hole-in-one on the seventh at the Everglades Club in Palm Beach, Florida. In tandem with another jumper, Englishman **Edward Royds-Jones**, age 95, parachutes out of a plane. Coach of the only team to win the NIT and the NCAA Tournament in the same year, **Nat Holman**, age 95, is asked what he thinks of Michael Jordan. His reply: "The name rings a bell but I can't place him, though I may know him by sight." Pilot **Stanley Wood**, age 96, continues to fly a Piper Cherokee Warrior. **Amos Alonzo Stagg**, age 96, runs laps around the fig trees in his backyard.

# AMOS ALONZO STAGG
continues to co-coach football
at Susquehanna.

In Athens, **Dimitrion Yordanidis**, age 98, runs a marathon in seven hours, thirty-three minutes—the oldest person to complete a marathon. **Otto Bucher**, age 99, makes a hole-in-one on the twelfth at La Manga golf club in Spain. **John Fleck's** hours in the pool pay off at the Senior Olympics when he sets a record for the one hundred meter freestyle at age 99.

**Ichijirou Araya** of Japan, age 100, climbs Mount Fuji. Refusing to play in senior leagues, **Papa John Venturello**, age 100, bowls on five teams and holds a 141 average. In Saint Petersburg, Florida, **George Bakewell**, age 100, plays softball with the Kids and the Kubs. He also appears in a Nike commercial, saying, "It's gotta be the shoes." **"Gamblin' Rose" Hamburger**, age 105, gets a new job: picking the winners at Aqueduct race park for the *New York Post*.

# INDEX

# INDEX

At age 6, DAVID LEWMAN sang on a series of records called *Let's Learn to Sing*. At age 35, he made his off-Broadway debut alongside George Wendt in a quasi-musical called *Wild Men*. At his current age (which he cannot disclose, as he recently moved to Los Angeles), he wrote this book. He has also written articles for *Nickelodeon* magazine, *Inside Chicago*, *Online Access*, and *Chicago Times*.

MARK ANDERSON illustrates and designs publications for a number of national and international clients. His illustrations have appeared in *Outside* magazine, *Chicago Magazine*, the *Chicago Tribune* and the *Washingtonian*. At age 33, this is his first book.